Katie's Guide to Bead Identification

Alphabet Beads
Available in a variety of styles, large-hole and small-hole.

E-Beads
Larger than seed beads but no larger than 4mm.

Gemstone Chips
Uneven pieces drilled for bead stringing.

Pony Beads
Short, cylindrial glass or plastic beads with large holes.

Bicone Beads
Beads with a cone shape on each end.

Embossed Beads
Textured beads that have a raised design.

Rondelles
Any ring-shaped bead. Often used as spacers.

Lampwork Glass Beads
Three-dimensional handmade glass beads.

Seed Beads
Tiny beads available in different sizes and colors. Size 10/0 is used for the projects in this book.

Bugle Beads
Tubular seed beads available in different lengths, styles and colors.

Faceted Beads
Glass or plastic beads which have many cuts on the sides to create a "diamond" effect.

Metal Spacers
Used to add interest to a design. Available in many shapes and sizes.

Cane Glass Beads
These look like pieces of striped glass.

Fiber Optic Beads
These have a reflective band across the center.

Silver-lined Beads
The inner part of this bead is lined with silver to create a reflective quality inside the glass. This technique is used for beads of many shapes, sizes and colors.

photographs not to scale

Beading Thread

A very thin thread used for stringing small, delicate beads. Use it with a beading needle and seed beads (see page 32).

Chain

Available in many styles and can add an elegant look to jewelry designs. To cut a chain, use flush cutters. Attach beads and clasps using eye pins, craft wire, split rings or jump rings.

Craft Wire

Available in a variety of colors and sizes. It is typically enamel-coated copper wire, which makes it inexpensive and easy to bend. The smaller the diameter, the higher the gauge number.

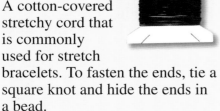

Elastic Cord

A cotton-covered stretchy cord that is commonly used for stretch bracelets. To fasten the ends, tie a square knot and hide the ends in a bead.

Flexible Beading Wire

Several miniature wires are twisted or braided together and covered with a nylon coating. Tiger Tail contains seven or fewer strands. More flexible wires include 19 or more strands.

Hemp Cord

Comes in a variety of sizes and finishes, from thread-weight to heavy rope. 20# test weight is the most commonly used for jewelry making and is used in this book. Hemp softens as it is worn, acquiring a comfortable, cottony feel.

Leather Cord

Available in several diameters and colors as well as in a faux leather. It works well with larger-hole beads. Use a bead-and-loop closure, cord ends or eye crimps to add a clasp.

Suede Lace

A flat cord that works well for jewelry designs. Its flatness tends to twist—this effect can be used to enhance a design or may be prevented with careful bead or knot placement. Use a bead-and-loop closure, cord ends or eye crimps to add a clasp.

Memory Wire

A special wire that retains its shape. It is made to fit the neck, wrist or finger and is sold by the loop or in continuous loops. Special memory wire shears are require to cut it—don't use your craft wire cutters, they'll be ruined. No clasps are necessary, but the ends can be finished by looping the end (against the natural curve) or gluing on special end caps (see page 3).

Satin, or Rattail, Cord

Available in several diameters and colors. It works well with larger-hole beads. When knotting it, pull the knots as tight as possible due to its slippery texture. Use a bead-and-loop closure, cord ends or eye crimps to add a clasp.

Silk Thread

Available in variouse sized and colors, it is used primarily for pearls and small gemstones. It is subject to abrasion so be sure the bead holes are smooth.

Stretch Plastic Cord

A thin, pliable cord used for making bracelets and many other types of jewelry. It is commonly translucent and may be used for "illusion" designs. To fasten the ends, tie a square knot or use crimp beads to attach a clasp.

photographs not to scale

In Katie's Beading Toolbox

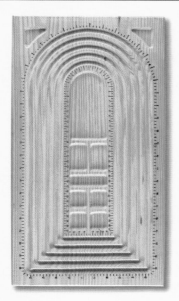

Bead Board
Use a bead board to plan your designs before you start stringing. It has guides for the placement of your beads and keeps them from rolling away!

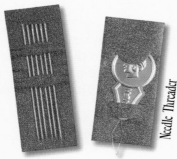

Needle Threader

Beading Needles
Use these when stringing beads onto thread. To make stringing easier, use long needles so that many beads will fit on the needle.

Chain Nose Pliers
Use these to make 90° angles, open and close jump rings and to hold loops while wrapping.

Crimping Pliers
These make crimp beads/tubes look slightly rounded. Place the crimp bead/tube in the inner jaw and squeeze hard. This creates a dent in the center of the bead. Place the crimp bead/tube in the outer jaws with the dent positioned horizontally. Squeeze gently to fold the bead or tube.

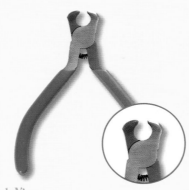

End Nippers
Cutters used to cut wire and findings. They create a close, even cut.

Flat Nose Pliers
Used primarily to open and close jump rings.

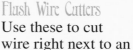

Flush Wire Cutters
Use these to cut wire right next to an object.

Memory Wire Shears
Use these specifically to cut memory wire. They can also be used to cut other wire, but the jaws will not make a close cut due to their design.

Round Nose Pliers
Use the tip of the jaws to make small loops and the back of the jaws to make large loops.

Wire Nippers
Cutters used to cut wire and findings. Also called side cutters because the blades are on the side of the pliers.

photographs not to scale

3

Bar Pins

Available in different sizes. Attach beads using craft wire or jewelry glue.

Bead Caps

Fit over the ends of a bead and add interest to a design. The cap should match the bead size (i.e., use a 6mm cap with a 6mm bead). No glue is needed, simply string one before and after the bead (opened toward the bead).

Beading Hoops

Wire hoops with a straight end and a looped end. String beads onto the hoop, then bend the straight end at a 90° angle to fasten it through the loop. Don't confuse these with earring hoops.

Bell Caps

These have a loop on one end and an opening on the other. Use jewelry glue to attach a bead inside the open end to convert the bead into a pendant.

Clip Barrettes

Available in several sizes. Use craft wire or jewelry glue to attach beads.

Cord Ends & Cord Caps

Use to attach cord or lacing to a clasp. For cord ends use chain nose pliers to flatten the first two coils against the cord. For cord caps, glue the cord ends inside the cap with jewelry glue.

Clasps

Barrel   **Hook & Eye**

Lanyard Hook   **Lobster**

Magnetic   **Snap**

Spring ring   **Toggle**

Torpedo

Crimp Beads

Crimp Tubes

Special beads and tubes that become flattened when squeezed with pliers. Use chain nose pliers to flatten them or crimping pliers to give them a more rounded look. Use two for extra strength.

Earrings Posts & Clip Earrings

Glue beads or rhinestones to the flat disc on the earring post or use an eye pin or craft wire to hang beads from the lower loop.

Ear Wires & Hoops

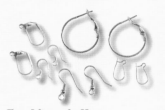

Available in different styles. Choose one that looks the best with your design.

Eye Crimps

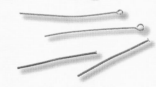

Use to attach cord or lacing to a clasp.

Head & Eye Pins

Lengths of wire with a loop head or a flat head, like a nail. Available in different lengths and materials.

Jump Rings

Circles of thick wire that are available in different sizes. Use them to attach charms and clasps, or connect several to make an extension chain.

Memory Wire End Caps

Use a 2-step epoxy glue to attach these to cut memory wire ends.

Multi-strand End Piece

Attach this to the end of a multi-strand design to hold the ends separate and to add a more professional look.

Tie Tack Pin Backs with Butterfly Clasps

Glue rhinestones or beads to the disc surface to create a pin. Use a smaller surface as needed.

Spacer Bars

Used to separate strands in a multiple strand design.

Split Rings

Available as large as a key ring and as small as a jump ring. Use small split rings in place of jump rings when extra security is needed.

What to Wear

When choosing jewelry to coordinate with your outfits (or vice versa), it may help to consider the following:

13" square knot choker, page 29

16" memory wire choker, page 19

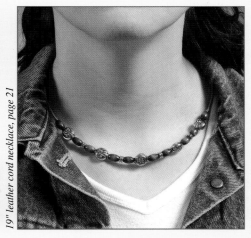

19" leather cord necklace, page 21

Chokers (13"-16") generally look better with round neck or boat neck shirts. If the pattern is repeated on the entire necklace, they may also be worn with collared shirts. They are not typically worn with turtlenecks.

16½" wire link necklace, page 16

Single or multiple strand necklaces with no pendant look good with round neck shirts and shirts with collars or jackets.

Necklaces with pendants and Y-necklaces are typically worn with lower-cut shirts and with shirts with a collar—if the collar is open enough to reveal the pendant.

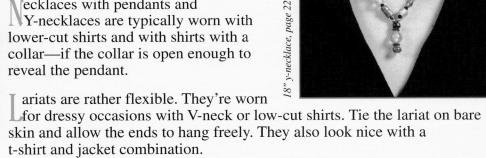

18" y-necklace, page 22

Lariats are rather flexible. They're worn for dressy occasions with V-neck or low-cut shirts. Tie the lariat on bare skin and allow the ends to hang freely. They also look nice with a t-shirt and jacket combination.

50" covered wood bead lariat, page 35

58" suede lariat with charms, page 8

50" patterned lariat, page 22

Of course, rules were made to be broken!

Katie's Easy Beaded Charms

Katie's Easy Beaded Charms

"**Just**" string your favorite bead, add an ear wire and voilà—you have a great pair of basic earrings. Head and eye pins make creating lots of different jewelry designs super simple. Base-metal (silver-plated brass, copper, etc.) findings work fine for most projects, but use sterling silver with more expensive or unique beads. Try the following projects to get started!"

Basic Techniques

Simple Eye Loop

1 With chain nose pliers, grasp the wire 1/4"-1/2" from the end. Turn the pliers to bend the wire back at a right angle.

2 With round nose pliers, grasp the very end of the wire. Roll the pliers upward to make the loop—let go and move the pliers if necessary to get a nice round loop.

3 Use the chain nose pliers to flatten and straighten the loop. It should sit centered on the wire end.

Wrapped Eye Loop

1 Grasp the wire 1" from one end with chain nose pliers. Bend back at a right angle, then use round nose pliers to grasp the wire 1/4" from the bend. Turn the pliers to form a loop—the wire ends should be parallel.

2 Hold the loop with chain nose pliers—be sure the base of the loop is visible. Wrap the wire end 3-4 times in a tight coil below the loop. Trim the excess wire.

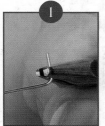
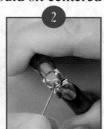

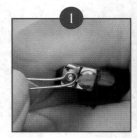

Beaded Charm Set

length: 15½"
16 assorted 4mm glass beads
eleven 1½" silver head pins
four 6mm silver jump rings
15½" silver ball chain necklace
2 silver ear wires
basic beaded charm supplies (see above)

necklace close-up

1 **Necklace:** String a single bead on two separate head pins. Make a wrapped loop (see above). String two beads on three separate head pins and make a wrapped loop above each top bead. Connect two jump rings and string one onto the necklace. Attach the beaded head pins to the bottom jump ring.

2 **Earrings:** Follow step 1 but string a single bead on four separate head pins and two beads on two separate head pins. Attach a jump ring to each ear wire. String two single-bead head pins and one double-bead pin onto each jump ring.

Charm Pin

length: 2"
4mm round glass beads: 4 turquoise, 6 blue
8mm round turquoise bead
three 9mm embossed silver butterfly beads
3 loop 2" silver safety pin
seven 1½" silver head pins
2" silver eye pin
basic beaded charm supplies (see page 7)

1 String a blue bead and a 4mm turquoise bead onto four spearate head pins. Make a wrapped loop (see page 7) above each top bead attaching two beaded charms to each outer loop on the safety pin.

2 String a blue bead, an 8mm turquoise bead and a blue bead onto the eye pin. Make a wrapped loop attaching it to the center loop on the safety pin. String each butterfly bead onto a head pin and make a wrapped loop attaching each to the bottom loop on the eye pin.

Suede Lariat with Charms

length: 58"
two 16mm handmade silver beads
gemstone beads: 10-12 carnelian chips, four 6mm turquoise rounds
4 turquoise e-beads
two 2" silver eye pins
two silver eye crimps
1½ yards of brown suede lacing
basic beaded charm supplies (see page 7)

1 Attach an eye crimp (see page 18) to each end of the suede lacing. String an e-bead, 2-3 carnelian chips, a silver bead, 2-3 more chips and an e-bead onto an eye pin.

2 Make a wrapped loop (see page 7) above the top bead attaching it to one end of the lacing. String a turquoise bead onto a head pin; make two. Make a wrapped loop above each attaching them to the bottom loop on the eye pin. Repeat for the other end of the lariat.

Beaded Key Chain

length: 1¾"
silver-lined turquoise glass beads: one 12mm cylinder, two 8mm round
e-beads: 2 clear, 1 turquoise
9mm embossed silver butterfly bead
three 1" silver head pins
2" silver eye pin
¾" silver key ring
basic beaded charm supplies (see page 7)

1 String a clear bead, the cylindrical turquoise bead and a clear e-bead onto the eye pin. Use the largest part of the round nose pliers to make a wrapped loop (see page 7) attaching it to the key ring.

2 String a turquoise e-bead and the butterfly onto a head pin. Make a wrapped loop attaching it to the bottom loop on the eye pin. String each round turquoise bead onto separate head pins. Make a wrapped loop attaching each to the bottom loop on the eye pin.

Wine Charms

six garden theme (or your choice) silver charms
5mm bicone beads (glass or plastic): 2 pink, 2 orange,
*   2 yellow, 2 green, 2 blue, 2 purple, 2 blue*
e-beads: 2 pink, 2 orange, 2 yellow, 2 green, 2 blue,
*   2 purple, 2 blue*
twenty-four 4mm round silver beads
6 silver beading hoops
6 silver jump rings
twelve ¾" silver head pins
Super Glue™
basic beaded charm supplies (see page 7)

1 String a pink bicone bead onto a head pin. Make a simple loop (see page 7) above the bead; make two. Attach the wheel barrow charm to a jump ring.

2 String a silver bead, a pink e-bead, a pink beaded head pin, a silver bead, the charm, a silver bead, a pink beaded eye pin, a pink e-bead and a silver bead onto a beading hoop. Use the chain nose pliers to bend the end of the hoop at an angle. Arrange the beads centered on the hoop and place a drop of glue on each outer bead. Repeat for each remaining color and charm.

Charm Bracelet

length: 7"
silver key charms: two ¾", one 1"
three 10mm round purple glass beads
6 purple e-beads
three 10mm embossed silver beads
three 4mm round silver beads
3 silver jump rings
six 2" silver head pins
7½" silver chain bracelet
basic beaded charm supplies (see page 7)

1 String a round silver bead and a purple glass bead on a head pin; make three. String an e-bead, an embossed bead and an e-bead on a head pin; make three.

2 Connect the beaded head pins to the bracelet with wrapped loops and the charms with jump rings as shown.

Braided Satin Cord Choker

length: 14"
green glass beads: one 10mm round, one 12mm oval
e-beads: 2 green, 2 black
one 6mm round hematite bead
five 4mm faceted gray glass beads
four 1½" silver head pins
8mm silver jump ring
three 15" lengths of 1mm black satin cord
2 silver coiled cord ends
silver lobster clasp
basic beaded charm supplies (see page 7)

1 Hold the satin cord ends together and place a cord end over them (see page 18). Attach the cord end to your work surface. Braid the cords together and attach a cord end. Attach the clasp to one cord end.

2 String three faceted beads onto a head pin and make a wrapped loop (see page 7). String two faceted beads and two green e-beads onto a head pin; make a wrapped loop. String a black e-bead and the oval green bead onto a head pin; make a wrapped loop. String the hematite bead, the round green bead and a black e-bead onto a head pin; make a wrapped loop.

3 Attach all of the beaded head pins to the jump ring. Attach the jump ring through the center of the braid.

Memory Wire Bracelet with Charms

length: 14½"
ten 8-10mm round clear silver-lined glass beads
five 10-12mm oval amber silver-lined glass beads
e-beads: 48 brown, 28 amber
silver rondelle spacers: twenty-four 4mm, ten 6mm fluted
2 loops of bracelet memory wire
fourteen 1½" silver head pins
basic beaded charm supplies (see page 7)

1 String two brown e-beads onto a head pin and make a wrapped loop (see page 7); make 12. String two amber e-beads onto a head pin and make a wrapped loop; make two. Make a loop on one end of the memory wire (see page 2) and string an amber beaded head pin before closing the loop.

2 String a 4mm spacer, two brown e-beads, a 4mm spacer and two amber e-beads onto the memory wire. String two brown beaded head pins, two amber e-beads, a 4mm spacer and two brown e-beads.

3 String a clear bead, a 6mm spacer, an amber bead, a 6mm spacer and a clear bead. Repeat steps two and three until all of the beads are used. Loop the end of the memory wire and string the remaining amber beaded head pin before closing the loop.

Stretch Cuff Bracelet

length: 8¼"
clear faceted glass beads: twenty-two 8mm discs with crosswise
holes, forty-four 6mm round, eighty-eight 4mm bicone
forty-four 4mm bicone purple glass beads
20" length of 0.5 clear stretch beading cord
twenty-two 1½" silver eye pins
adhesive tape
basic beaded charm supplies (see page 7)

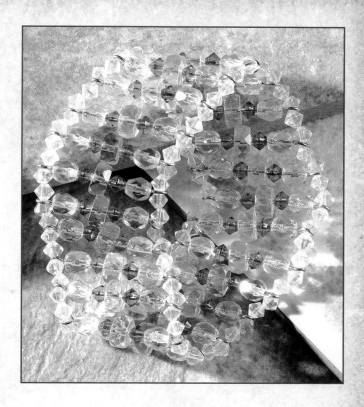

1 String a 6mm clear, a purple, an 8mm clear, a purple and a 6mm clear bead onto each eye pin. Make a simple loop (see page 7) on each.

2 Cut the cord in half. Tape one end of each length to your work surface. String two bicones on one strand and one end of a beaded eye pin. Repeat this pattern until all of the pins have one end on the cord. Place a piece of tape over the end.

3 Repeat the bead stringing pattern for the other length of cord using the opposite end of the eye pins. After all of the pins are strung, tie the cord ends into a square knot (see page 26). Pull the cord ends gently to tighten the knot before trimming any excess cord.

Three Pairs of Earrings

Simple Beaded Earrings, ⅝"
four 8mm faceted clear glass disc
beads with crosswise holes
two 8mm round faux pearls
two 1½" silver head pins
2 silver ear wires
basic beaded charm supplies (see
page 7)

Simple Beaded Earrings
For each: String a disc bead, a pearl and a disc bead onto a head pin. Make a wrapped loop (see page 7) attaching it to an ear wire.

Extended Drop Earrings, 1¼"
clear faceted glass beads: four 8mm
round, two 10mm round
8 silver jump rings
six 2" silver eye pins
2 silver ear wires
basic beaded charm supplies (see
page 7)

Extended Drop Earrings
For Each: String two 8mm beads and a 10mm bead each onto separate head pins. Make a wrapped loop on each pin. Connect four jump rings (see page 18) into a chain, then attach it to an ear wire. Attach an 8mm head pin to the first jump ring and one to the second. Attach the 10mm head pin to the bottom jump ring.

Beaded Earrings with Drop, 1⅜"
faceted clear glass beads: two 8mm disc beads
with crosswise holes, two 8mm round
four 6mm round faux pearls
two 2" silver head pins
two 1½" silver eye pins
2 silver ear wires
basic beaded charm supplies (see page 7)

Beaded Earrings with Drop
For each: String a pearl, a disc bead and a pearl onto an eye pin. Make a simple loop attaching it to an ear wire. String a round faceted bead onto a head pin. Make a wrapped loop attaching it to the bottom of the eye pin.

Katie's Introduction to Wire-Wrapping

Katie's Introduction to Wire-Wrapping

"Craft wire is available in a range of diameters, called "gauges." The larger the diameter, the smaller the gauge. Thus, 18-gauge wire is heavier than 28-gauge wire. Some of the same techniques for head and eye pins can be used to bend craft wire.

Wear safety glasses or hold your hand over wire ends as you cut them. The wire bits fly fast and are sharp! Use chain nose pliers to tuck in any sharp, exposed wire ends. Note the wire's natural curve and work in that direction."

Basic Supplies
- round nose pliers
- chain nose pliers
- flat nose pliers
- wire nippers
- ruler

Basic Techniques

Flat Spiral

1 Place the tip of round nose pliers at the wire end and turn to make a tiny loop.

2 Grasp the loop with flat nose pliers. Turn the pliers, holding the wire flat and feeding it into the spiral.

Figure-8 Eye

1 Cut a 2" length of wire. Place the wire at the center of round nose pliers and roll the pliers to make a loop. Move the pliers to grasp the wire just below the loop and bend the wire around the pliers in the opposite direction to make the figure-8.

2 Use flat nose pliers to hold the second loop while you wrap the wire end 2-3 times around the center of the figure-8. Trim any excess wire.

Wire-wrapped Bead Caps

1 Make a simple eye loop (see page 7) or spiral on one wire end. Place a bead on the wire so the straight end extends upward.

2 Make a simple eye loop ⅛" above the bead. Wrap the wire end down around the wire below the loop.

3 Continue wrapping down onto the bead, making each ring slightly larger than the previous one to produce a conical cap. Wrap carefully so each wire ring lies flat against the bead—if you wrap too tightly, the wire will bunch up.

4 To finish, trim the wire end and form it into a loop or spiral, or wrap the free wire end downward around the bead.

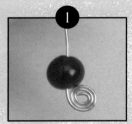

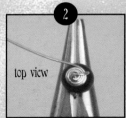

top view

Wire-Wrapped Hair Clip

2 yards of 24-gauge black craft wire
3¾" metal clip barrette
clear e-beads with color inside: 12 purple, 12 orange, 9 pink,
*   9 blue, 9 green*
basic wire-wrapping supplies (see page 13)

1 Place one end of the wire through the hole in one end of the barrette and wrap it three times. Wrap the wire around the wide end of the barrette three times.

2 String three purple beads onto the wire and wrap it around the barrette three more times. Repeat the three-bead, three-wrap pattern alternating colors as shown. At the end, wrap the wire through the hole three times. Tuck the wire ends into the wires on the back of the barrette.

Twisted Wire Pin

2½" wide
1 yard of 24-gauge black   *jewelry glue*
*   craft wire*   *super glue*
1" antique silver oval bead   *basic wire-wrapping supplies*
6 black e-beads   *   (see page 13)*
½" bar pin

1 Glue the pin back to the silver bead with jewelry glue and let dry. Cut the wire into three equal lengths. Fold each length in half and twist the ends together until each length is completely twisted. String the lengths through the silver bead.

2 String an e-bead onto both ends of each wire and place them next to the silver bead. Make a spiral (see page 13) one each wire end. Place a drop of super glue in each e-bead.

Wire-Wrapped Memory Choker

length: 20"
2 coninuous loops of necklace memory wire
52 assorted 6mm pastel alphabet beads
55 assorted clear e-beads with color inside
24" length of 24-gauge silver craft wire
memory wire shears
basic wire-wrapping supplies (see page 13)

1 Use round nose pliers to make a loop at one end of the memory wire. String two e-beads onto the wire. String the letter "A" and an e-bead. Repeat until all of the beads are used. String the last e-bead onto the wire. Make a loop on the end of the wire 1" from the last bead.

2 Wrap the craft wire end in a ½" coil between the two e-beads at the end of the necklace. Wrap the wire diagonally around the necklace to reach the other end. Make another ½" coil between the last two e-beads. Trim any excess wire.

Wire-Wrapped Necklace

length: 18½"
*gold glass beads: four 12mm square,
    six 8mm bicone, one 15mm
    diamond*
*ten 6" lengths of 24-gauge gold craft
    wire*
two 6" lengths of gold necklace chain

gold head pin
2 gold jump rings
gold spring ring clasp and tag
*basic wire-wrapping supplies (see
    page 13)*

1 Make a wrapped loop (see page 7) and string a square bead
onto a wire length. Make another wrapped loop (see photo
A). Form a loop on the front and back of the bead (see photo
B). Wrap the wire ends around the wrapped loops and trim any
excess. Repeat with each square bead.

2 String a bicone bead on a length of wire. Make a bead cap
(see page 13) on one end, connecting one end of one length
of the necklace chain. Make a bead cap on the other end of the
bicone bead, attaching it to a square bead from step 1.

3 String a bicone bead on a length of wire and make a bead cap
on one end, attaching it to the square bead in step 2. Make
a bead cap on the other end of the bead, attaching it to a square
bead from step 1. Repeat steps 2-3 for the other side of the
necklace.

4 String the diamond bead onto a length of wire. Make a
wrapped loop on one end and wrap the wire end down
around the bead. String a bicone bead on a length of wire and
make a bead cap on one end, connecting the two bottom square
beads. Make a bead cap on the other end, attaching it to the
wrapped loop on the diamond bead. Use round nose pliers to
make a figure-8 shape below the diamond bead and a small loop
below the center of the figure-8 as shown.

5 String a bicone bead onto the head pin and make a bead cap,
attaching it to the loop below the figure-8. Use the jump rings
to attach the clasp and tag to the chain.

Wire-Wrapped Bracelet

length: 8"
eleven 8mm round faux pearls
44" length of 24-gauge silver craft wire
silver spring ring clasp and tag
basic wire-wrapping supplies (see page 13)

1 Cut the wire into 4" lengths. Make a wrapped
loop (see page 7) 1" from one end of a piece
of wire. String a pearl onto the wire, then make a
wrapped loop on the other end and attach half of the
clasp.

2 Repeat for each bead, linking the previous one
on the bracelet. Attach half of the clasp to the
end before wrapping the final loop.

Sprial Necklace & Earrings

Necklace, 18":
12" length of 20-gauge silver craft wire
12mm red/silver barrel glass bead
3 red e-beads
18" silver ball chain necklace
silver jump rings: 6mm, 9mm
basic wire-wrapping supplies (see page 13)

Earrings, 1³/₄":
18" of 20-gauge silver craft wire
two 13mm red/silver barrel glass beads
2 silver post earrings
jewelry glue
basic wire-wrapping supplies (see page 13)

1 **Necklace:** Cut three 4" lengths of craft wire. Make a loose spiral (see page 13) on the end of one wire. String a barrel bead and make a wrapped loop (see page 7) above it. Make a loose spiral on the end of one wire length. String an e-bead and make a wrapped loop. Make a loose spiral on the remaining wire and string two e-beads. Make a wrapped loop at the top and wrap the wire end down around the beads. Attach the top loop of each beaded charm to the 9mm jump ring. Attach the 9mm jump ring to the necklace chain with the 6mm jump ring.

2 **For each earring:** Cut a 3" length of craft wire. Make a tight spiral, then use the round nose pliers to make a loop hanger as shown. Glue the spiral to an earring post and let it dry completely. Cut a 6" length of wire and make a loose spiral on one end. String a barrel bead and make a wrapped loop. Wrap the wire end down around the bead. Attach the wrapped bead to the loop on the spiral.

Wire Link Necklace

length: 16½"
pink beads: eleven 6mm round fiber optic, thirteen 6mm faceted glass, three 4mm bicone
twenty 4mm round silver beads
triangular silver pendant with three lower loops

50" length of 24-gauge silver craft wire
4 silver head pins
2 silver split rings
silver lobster clasp
basic wire-wrapping supplies (see page 13)

1 Cut ten 2" lengths of wire. String a faceted bead on each one and make a wrapped loop (see page 7) on each end. Set them aside for step 2.

2 Cut five 3" lengths of wire. String a silver bead, a fiber optic and a silver bead. Make a wrapped loop on one end attaching it to the top loop on the pendant. Make a wrapped loop on the other end attaching it to a bead from step 1. Alternate fiber optic sets with faceted beads until five of the faceted beads are used. Attach a split ring to the end.

3 Repeat step 2 for the other side of the necklace. Attach the clasp to the end. String a faceted bead and the bicone beads onto a head pin. Make a wrapped loop attaching it to the top loop and the center of the pendant. String two faceted beads and a fiber optic bead on separate head pins. Make a wrapped loop at the top of each attaching them to the lower loops on the pendant as shown.

Katie's Basic Bead Stringing

Basic Techniques

Attaching an Eye Crimp

Lay the strand or strands in the open side of an eye crimp, extending away from the eye. Use flat nose pliers to flatten each crimp side over the strands.

Attaching a Cord End

Place one end of the cord inside the coiled cord end. Use chain nose pliers to flatten the first one or two rings of the coil against the cord. Pull gently on the cord to make sure it is secure.

Crimp Beads & Tubes

Crimp beads and tubes become flattened when squeezed with pliers. They're great for holding ends together or as spacers. To use, place the bead exactly where you want it, then use flat nose pliers to squeeze it. There are special crimping pliers on the market which will close the crimp more securely and rounds the bead, smoothing sharp edges often left by simply using flat nose pliers.

Jump Rings

1 With flat nose pliers, grasp the ring on each side of the opening and rotate one pair of pliers to open the ring like a hinge. Don't pull the ends away from each other, as that will distort the shape and you'll never get the ring to close properly again.

2 To connect jump rings, open one ring as in step 1, then hook on the second jump ring.

3 Use the flat nose pliers to close the first jump ring.

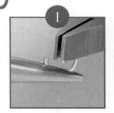  

Single Strand Necklace

length: 18"
faceted glass beads: fifty-four 5mm black, ten 8mm clear
gold beads: 52 seed beads, eight 6mm fluted
six 8mm gold bead caps
18" length of flexible beading wire
2 gold crimp beads
gold barrel clasp
crimping pliers

1 String a crimp bead ½" from the end of the wire. String half of the clasp on the wire and place the end back into the crimp bead; flatten it closed (see above). String a 5mm black bead and a gold seed bead. Repeat until half of the black beads are used.

2 String a 6mm gold, a clear, a 6mm gold, a clear, a 6mm gold and a clear bead.

3 String a bead cap with the opening toward the next bead, an 8mm black, a bead cap, a clear, a gold and a clear bead. Repeat twice then string a gold, a clear and a gold bead. Repeat step 1 in the reverse order so the necklace is symmetrical.

Illusion Necklace

length: 16"
fifteen 4mm pink glass bicone beads
32 silver crimp beads
16" length of flexible beading wire
silver barrel clasp
chain nose pliers
crimping pliers

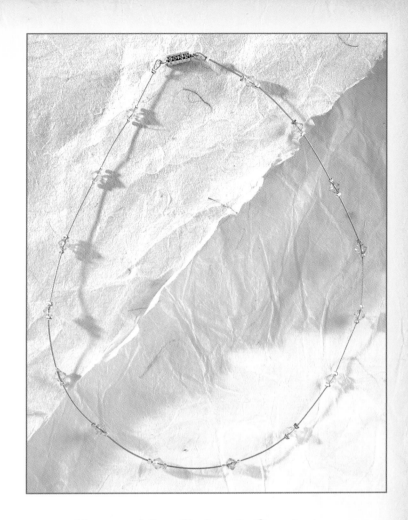

1 String a crimp bead ½" from the end of the wire. String half of the clasp onto the wire and place the end back into the crimp bead; flatten it closed (see page 17). String a crimp bead, a bicone bead and a crimp bead. Adjust the beads so the glass bead is 1" from the clasp. Flatten the crimp bead on each side.

2 Repeat the pattern, adjusting the beads so each glass bead is 1" from the next. At the end of the necklace string a crimp bead ½" from the end of the wire. String the other half of the clasp onto the wire and place the end back into the crimp bead; flatten it closed.

Memory Wire Choker & Bracelet

Choker, 16":
1½ continuouse loops of necklace memory wire
12mm antique silver bead
8mm round beads: 2 silver, 2 black
122 black e-beads
memory wire shears
round nose pliers

Bracelet, 16½":
2½ continuouse loops of bracelet memory wire
nine 6mm round silver beads
100 black e-beads
memory wire shears
round nose pliers

1 **For the necklace:** Make a loop on one end (see page 2) of the wire. String fifty-seven e-beads, a round silver bead and four e-beads. String an 8mm black bead, the antique silver bead and an 8mm black bead. String four e-beads, a round silver and 57 e-beads. Make a loop on the end of the wire.

2 **For the bracelet:** Make a loop on one end of the wire. String ten e-beads and a silver bead. Repeat until all of the beads are used. Make a loop on the end of the wire.

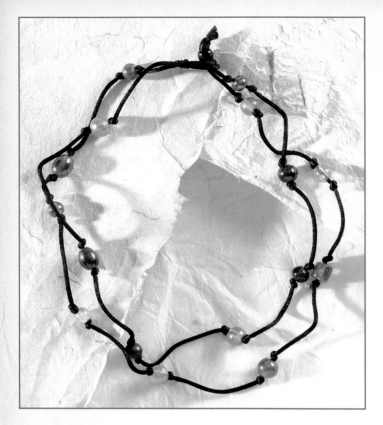

Knotted Cord Necklace

length: 22¹/₂"
sixteen 8-14mm assorted
  large-hole glass beads
black pony bead
1³/₄ yards of 2mm black satin
  cord

6" length of 24-gauge black
  craft wire
chain nose pliers
scissors

1 Cut the cord in half. Hold the lengths together and fold the ends to make a ³/₄" loop. Secure the loop by wrapping the wire around the base. Use chain nose pliers to press the wire ends into the cord.

2 On one strand tie an overhand knot (see page 26) 2" from the loop. String a bead and tie another knot. On the other strand tie an overhand knot 1" from the loop. String a bead and tie another knot. Continue stringing beads and tying knots on each strand 2" between each bead.

3 After all of the glass beads are used, string the pony bead onto both strands. Adjust the strands so one is longer than the other then tie them in an overhand knot. Use pliers to tighten the knot. Trim any excess cord.

Katie says: "The key to knotting cord is to always tie the knots in the same direction. If the first knot you make is around your left hand and you pull the knot through from the bottom of the cord, make all the knots the same way."

Chunky Bracelet Set

length: 5¹/₂" each
10mm etched plastic bicone
  beads: 3 white, 2 turquoise,
  3 rust
10mm etched plastic pillow
  beads: 3 white
12mm etched plastic cylinder
  beads: 3 white, 3 turquoise,
  3 rust

10mm etched plastic washers: 8
  white, 15 turquoise, 9 rust
black wooden beads: fourteen
  10mm round, six 12mm
  cylinder
48" length of heavy black elastic
  cord
scissors

1 **Bicone bracelet:** Cut a 16" length of cord and fold it in half. Hold the strands together and string a round black bead, a white washer and a turquoise bicone bead. Repeat the pattern alternating colors as shown. Tie the ends of the cord into a square knot (see page 26). Trim any excess and push the knot into the nearest wood bead.

2 **Cylinder bracelet:** Cut a 16" length of cord and fold it in half. Hold the strands together and string a black cylinder, a white washer, a rust cylinder and a white washer. Repeat the pattern alternating colors as shown. Tie the ends into a square knot. Trim any excess and push the knot into the nearest wood bead.

3 **Pillow bracelet:** Cut a 16" length of cord and fold it in half. Hold the strands together and string a round black bead, a rust washer, a turquoise cylinder and a rust washer. String a black round bead, a turquoise washer, a pillow and a turquoise washer. Repeat the pattern alternating colors as shown. Tie the ends into a square knot. Trim any excess and push the knot into the nearest wood bead.

Leather Cord Necklace

length: 19"

five 10mm embossed silver
  beads
four 6mm silver spacer beads
ten 9mm oval wooden beads
18" length of 1mm brown
  leather cord

3" length of 24-gauge silver
  craft wire
2 silver eye crimps
silver barrel clasp
chain nose pliers
wire nippers

1 Attach an eye crimp (see page 18) to one end of the
  cord. String a wooden bead, and embossed bead,
a wood bead and a spacer bead. Repeat the pattern as
shown until all of the beads are used. Attach an eye
crimp to the end of the necklac. Attach half of the clasp
to each side of the necklace.

2 Arrange the beads so they are centered on the cord.
  Cut the wire in half and wrap each length in a tight
coil around the cord on each side of the beads. Use
chain nose pliers to press the wire ends into the cord.

Katie says: "Wrapping wire
around the cord on each side
of the beads prevents them
from sliding and keeps the
clasp in the back."

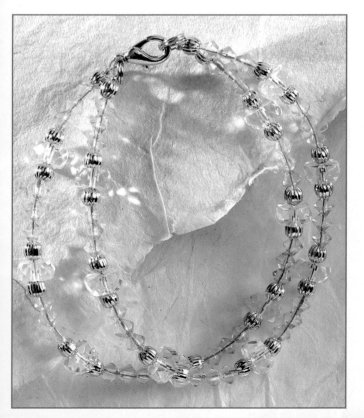

Double Strand Bracelet

length: 8"

forty-eight 5mm pink glass bicone beads
fourteen 8mm clear faceted rondelle glass beads
thirty-two 5mm round fluted silver beads
two 8" lengths of flexible beading wire
4 silver crimp beads
2 silver split rings
silver lobster clasp
crimping pliers

1 String a crimp bead ½" from the end of one wire.
  String a split ring onto the wire and place the end
back into the crimp bead; flatten it closed (see page 18).

2 String a silver bead, three pink beads, a silver bead
  and a clear bead; repeat for a total of seven sets.
String three pink beads, a silver bead and a crimp bead.
String a split ring onto the wire and place the end back
into the crimp bead; flatten it closed.

3 Repeat step 1 for the second strand. Attach the clasp
  to one end of the bracelet.

Y-Necklace

length: 18"
nine 8-12mm assorted glass beads
ninety-eight 5mm A/B finish* black bicone beads
six 4mm round silver beads
two 8mm silver rondelles
20" length of flexible beading wire
2 silver crimp beads
silver toggle clasp
crimping pliers

1 Divide the assorted glass beads into three sets of three. One set should contain a 12mm bead and two smaller beads of equal size.

2 String a glass bead onto the center of the wire. Hold the wire ends together and string a rondelle, a 12mm bead, a rondelle and a glass bead. String a silver bead onto each strand.

3 On each strand string a black bead, a glass bead, a black bead, a glass bead, a black bead and a glass bead. String a black bead and two silver beads onto each strand. String half of the remaining black beads onto each strand.

4 String a crimp bead ½" from the end of each wire. String half of the clasp onto each wire and place the ends back into the crimp beads; flatten each closed (see page 17).

Patterned Lariat

length: 50"
5mm faceted glass beads: 72 AB finish* black, 72 gray
clear faceted glass beads: two 10mm, twenty-four 6mm
185 silver-lined clear e-beads
50" length of flexible beading wire
2 silver crimp beads
crimping pliers

1 String a crimp bead onto one end of the wire and flatten it closed (see page 17). String a 10mm clear bead. String six black beads, a 6mm clear bead, six gray beads and a 6mm clear bead; repeat this pattern for a total of six sets.

2 String all of the e-beads. Repeat step 1 in the reverse order so the lariat is symmetrical. String a 10mm clear bead and a crimp bead. Flatten it closed and trim any excess wire.

*AB finish = Aurora Borealis is a shiny rainbow-like finish
added to glass beads

Beaded Necklace Wire

length: 15"
round wooden beads: two 8mm, two 12mm
silver beads: 14mm embossed cylinder, two 6mm round,
   two 8mm rondelles
silver necklace wire with removable ball clasp

1 Remove the ball clasp from the wire. String a 6mm silver, an 8mm wood bead, a silver rondelle and a 12mm wood bead.

2 String the embossed silver bead. Repeat step 1 in reverse order so the necklace is symmetrical.

K atie suggests: "Necklace wires are a flexible design element that makes it easy to change beads frequently."

Knotted Cord Anklet

length: 7"+
large-hole beads: 20mm silver embossed tube, four 6mm round silver,
   four 8mm round gray
14" length of black leather cord
chain nose pliers

1 String the tube bead onto the cord. String a gray bead, a silver bead, a gray bead and a silver bead on each side of the tube.

2 Center the beads on the cord. Tie each strand around the other in an overhand knot (see page 26). Use the pliers to tighten the knots if necessary.

K atie offers: "The knots make this anklet instantly adjustable. Use this technique for necklaces and bracelets too!"

Cotton Cord Keychain

length: 3"
two 15mm large-hole embossed silver beads
two 6mm round large-hole silver beads
12" length of black cotton cord
¾" silver key ring
scissors

1 Fold the cord in half through the key ring. Leave a ½" loop and knot the cords together in an overhand knot (see page 26). String the cord ends through opposite sides of an embossed bead. Repeat with the other embossed bead.

2 Tie the ends together. Sting a 6mm bead on each strand and tie an overhand knot in each cord end.

Beaded Leather Anklet

length: 10½"
alphabet beads: 1 red heart, letters to spell "to bead"
4 silver-lined red e-beads
two 3¼" lengths of 1mm black leather cord
3½" length of flexible beading wire
2 silver crimp beads
4 silver coiled cord ends
silver barrel clasp
chain nose pliers
crimping pliers

1 Place a cord end on each end of the leather cords (see page 18). Attach one end of each cord to half of the clasp.

2 String a crimp bead ½" from the end of the wire. String a cord end onto the wire and place the end back into the crimp bead; flatten it closed. String the e-beads and the alphabet beads as shown. String a crimp bead attaching the remaining cord end; flatten it closed.

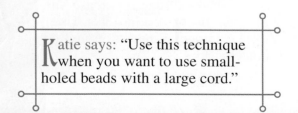

Katie says: "Use this technique when you want to use small-holed beads with a large cord."

Beginning Macramé With Katie

"Macramé is the art of knotting cord or string in patterns to make decorative articles. The pieces in this section are natural-looking and easy to make.

Basic Supplies
• scissors
• ruler

Hemp is preferred to other fiber cords for macramé because it knots easily and holds them well without glue. It is also smooth enough to be comfortable against the skin. Jute cord is similar in appearance but too scratchy to wear. Hemp comes in a variety of sizes and finishes, from thread-weight to heavy rope. Two sizes are commonly used for making knotted and braided jewelry: 20# test (about 1-1½mm) and 45-50# test (about 2mm)."

Basic Techniques

Overhand Knot

An overhand knot is tied in a single strand, or—more often—in a group of strands held together. It is most often used to begin or end a piece and is one of the simplest knots.

Half Knot

A half knot joins two strands. Wrap the right strand first over, then behind, then over the left strand. When repeated, this knot creates a tight spiral effect called a half knot sinnet.

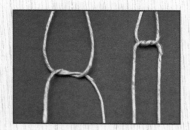

Square Knot (without center cords)

A square knot consists of two half knots tied in opposite directions. Wrap the right strand over, behind, and over the left strand. Bring the same strand (now on the left) behind, over and behind the right strand. Pull the ends in opposite directions to tighten them—be careful not to let the knot twist. When repeated, this knot creates a flat ribbon or square knot sinnet.

Square Knot (with center cords)

This knot identical to a square knot, except the knots are tied around the inner stands, which usually have beads strung on them.

Alternating Square Knot

1. This technique requires eight strands. To preserve the lacy look, don't pull the knots too tight. Secure the strands and separate them so they lay side by side.

2. Divide the strands into two groups of four. In each group, tie a square knot with the two outer strands over the two center strands.

3. Bring the two left strands of the right group and the two right strands of the left group to the center, dropping the two outer strands on each side.

4. Tie a square knot with the two outer strands over the two center strands. This completes one unit. Repeat from step 1 to the desired length.

Square Knot Sinnet

1. In a square knot sinnet, only the outer strands are worked; there may be none, one, two (usually) or more unused inner strands.

2. Make a half knot, with the left strand passing in front of the unused strands and the right passing behind, so that the unused strands are enclosed in a loop. Make another half knot with the right strand passing in front—this completes a square knot. Continue for the desired length.

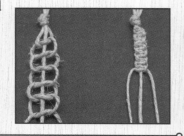

Guy's Half Knot Choker

length: 17½"
5 yards of 20# test hemp cord
six 8mm round large-hole hematite-look beads
12mm round large-hole black bead
basic macramé supplies (see page 26)

1 Cut the hemp into 4-yard and 1-yard lengths. Hold the cord centers together and fold them in half. Leave ½" and tie an overhand knot (see page 26). Arrange the strands so the long ones are on the outside and the short ones on the inside. Use the outer strands to tie half knots for 2". Hold the inner strands together and string an 8mm bead. Repeat the 2" of knots/one bead pattern for a total of six sets.

2 Use the outer strands to tie half knots for 2" then string the 12mm bead onto all of the strands. Tie the ends into an overhand knot. To fasten the necklace, slip the loop over the 12mm bead.

Red & Purple Bracelet

length: 7½"
2 yards of 20# test hemp cord
glass beads: two 8mm faceted red, two 8mm faceted
*   purple, two 10mm silver/red*
basic macramé supplies (see page 26)

1 Cut the hemp into 1½-yard and ½-yard lengths. Hold the cord centers together and fold them in half. Leave ½" and tie an overhand knot (see page 26). Arrange the strands so the long ones are on the outside and the short ones on the inside. Use the outer strands to tie half knots for 2".

2 Hold the inner strands together and string a red faceted bead. Tie a square knot with the outer strands. String a purple bead on the inner strands and tie a square knot with the outer strands. String a red/silver bead on the inner strands and tie a square knot with the outer strands. String a purple bead on the inner strands and tie a square knot with the outer strands. String a red faceted bead on the inner strands and tie a square knot with the outer strands. Tie 2" of half knots and string a red/silver bead on the inner strands. Tie all the strands in an overhand knot.

Men's Bracelet

beaded length: 9½"

3 yards of 1mm black leather cord
15 silver pony beads

chain nose pliers
basic macramé supplies (see page 26)

Cut the leather into 2⅓-yard and 24" lengths. Hold the cord centers together and tie an overhand knot (see page 26) making a ¾" loop. Arrange the strands so the long ones are on the outside and the short ones on the inside. Tie the outer strands in a square knots over the inner strands. String a pony bead onto the inner strands and tie the outer strands in a square knot. Repeat until all of the beads are used. Tie a final square knot then tie all of the strands in an overhand knot. Use the pliers to tighten the knot.

Katie suggests: "Convert this pattern into a women's bracelet by finishing it at 7" or 8". For a man's choker, double the materials."

Leather & Cotton Keychain

length: 4½"

24" length of 1mm black unwaxed cotton cord
24" length of 1mm brown leather cord
1¼" gold key ring
basic macramé supplies (see page 26)

Hold the cords together and place the key ring on them 8" from one end. Tie the cords in an overhand knot (see page 26). Arrange the strands so the long strands are on the outside, and the short strands on the inside. Tie the outer strands in six square knots around the inner strands. Tie all of the strands in an overhand knot.

Leather Choker

beaded length: 14"

3 yards of 1mm leather cord
large-hole wooded beads: fifty-two 8mm round, one 24mm tube
basic macramé supplies (see page 26)

1 Cut the cord in half. Hold the two lengths together and tie an overhand knot (see page 26) 6" from one end. String a round bead onto each strand. Tie the strands together in a square knot. Repeat for a total of 26 beads and 13 knots.

2 String the strand ends through opposite ends of the tube bead. Adjust the bead so it's straight and tie a square knot. String a round bead onto each strand and tie the strands together in a square knot. Repeat until all of the beads are used. Tie the ends in a overhand knot. To fasten the choker, tie the strands together in a square knot.

Suede Choker

beaded length: 14½"
3⅓ yards of brown suede lace
sixteen 12mm large-hole wooden barrel beads
basic macramé supplies (see page 26)

Cut the suede into one 24" length and two 48" lengths. Hold the cord ends together and tie them in an overhand knot (see page 26) 4" from the end. Arrange the strands so the long ones are on the outside and the short one is on the inside. Leave ½" and tie the long strands in a square knot around the short strand. String a bead on the inner strand then tie the long strands in a square knot, leaving the outer strands loose for a lacey look. Repeat until all of the beads are used. Tie an overhand knot at the end and trim the ends to 4".

Square Knot Anklet

length: 10"
4⅝ yards of 20# test hemp cord
12mm wooden barrel bead
2 silver coiled cord ends
lanyard hook clasp
needle nose pliers
paint pens: pink, green
basic macramé supplies (see page 26)

Cut the hemp into one 20" and two 2-yard lengths. Hold the cord centers together and fold them in half. Place the fold inside a cord end (see page 18). Arrange the strands so the long ones are on the outside and the short ones on the inside. Tie the outer strands in square knots (see page 26) around the inner strands for 4". String the bead onto the inner strands and tie the outer strands in square knots around the inner strands for 4". Trim the ends to ½" and place them in the remaining cord end. Use the pens to paint a flower on the bead.

Square Knot Choker

length: 13"
9 yards of 20#
  test hemp cord
wooden beads:
  2 light brown
  10mm barrel,
  dark brown
  16mm bicone,
  dark brown
  14mm round
basic macramé
  supplies (see
  page 26)

1. Cut the hemp into a 1-yard and two 4-yard lengths. Hold the cord centers together and tie them in an overhand knot (see page 26) to make a ¾" loop. Arrange the strands so the long ones are on the outside and the short ones on the inside. Tie the long strands in square knots around the short strands for 4¼". Leave a ¼" space and tie another square knot.

2. String a light brown bead onto the inside strands and tie the outer strands in a square knot. String the dark brown bicone bead onto the inside strands and tie the outer strands in a square knot. String a light brown bead onto the inside strands and tie the outer strands in a square knot. Leave a ¼" space and tie another square knot.

3. Tie the long strands in square knots around the short strands for 4¾". String the round bead on all of the strands then tie them in an overhand knot. Trim the ends to 1" long.

Alternating Square Knot Choker

length: 16"
12 yards of 20# test hemp cord
*wooden large-hole beads: four 8mm round, 12mm barrel,
16mm barrel*
basic macramé supplies (see page 26)

1 Cut the hemp into four 3-yard lengths. Hold the cord centers together and tie an overhand knot (see page 26) making a 1" loop. Tie alternating square knots for 5½", ending with a center knot.

2 String an 8mm bead onto the two center strands and tie them in a square knot. Tie three alternating square knots, ending with a center knot. String an 8mm bead onto the two center strands and tie them in a square knot. Tie a left and a right square knot.

3 Hold the four center strands together and string the 16mm bead. Tie three alternating knots. Repeat step 2. Tie alternating square knots for 5½" then string the 12mm bead onto all of the strands. Tie an overhand knot and trim the ends to 1". To fasten, slip the end bead through the loop.

Badge Lanyard

length: 30"
11 yards of 20# test hemp cord
six 6mm round large-hole wooden beads
silver eye crimp
two 6mm silver split rings
silver lanyard hook
basic macramé supplies (see page 26)

1 Cut the hemp into a 2-yard, 8½-yard and 12" lengths. Set the 12" length aside for step 3. Arrange the strands so the long strands are on the outside and the short strands are inside. Leave 2", then tie square knots (see page 26) for 1½" with the outside strands. Tie half knots for ¼" to make one full twist, then tie square knots for 1½". String a bead onto the inside strands and tie the outside strands in half knots for 1" to make two full twists.

2 Repeat the pattern from step 1 until all of the beads are used. Tie half knots for 1". Cut the stand ends to 2" and secure them in the eye crimp (see page 18).

3 Tie the 12" length in a square knot around the lanyard ¼" from where the two ends meet. Tie square knots to cover the eye crimp. After the last knot, wrap the ends to the back and tie a square knot to secure. Attach two split rings together, then attach one to the eye crimp and the other to the hook.

Katie's Simple Seed Beads

"**Seed beads** are available in a myriad of colors and sizes. The following projects use size 10/0 beads. There are approximately 16 beads per inch and 90 beads per gram. How many should you buy? Don't worry, for each project I've rounded up the quantity to the nearest 0.5 gram. Seed beads are so tiny that sometimes the holes are difficult to see. Make sure there is good lighting over your workspace and consider using a magnifier."

Basic Supplies

- beading needle
- The Ultimate! glue
- scissors
- optional: magnifier

Basic Techniques

Stringing Seed Beads

Dip the needle into the beads instead of picking them up with your fingers.

Knotting with Seed Beads

To make a knot right next to the beads, tie a loose overhand knot (see page 26). Place the needle tip inside the knot and push it next to the beads. Remove the needle and tighten the knot.

Seed Bead Bobby Pins

seed beads: 12 turquoise, 10 silver, 28 silver-lined blue
7mm acrylic rhinestones: 2 turquoise, 2 blue
4 silver bobby pins with 7mm disc

four 6" lengths of 24-gauge silver craft wire
wire nippers
chain nose pliers
basic seed bead supplies (see above)

1 **For each blue bobby pin:** Wrap a length of wire around a pin twice, close to the disc. String a blue bead and wrap the wire diagonally around the pin. String another bead and adjust it so it is next to the previous bead. Continue stringing beads until half of them are used. Wrap the wire end around the pin twice. Use chain nose pliers to press the wire ends to the pin. Glue a blue rhinestone to the disc.

2 **For each turquoise bobby pin:** Follow the directions for the blue bobby pins alternating turquoise and silver beads. Glue a turquoise rhinestone to the disc.

Seed Bead Brooch

length: 2½"
140 green seed beads (2 grams)
16mm oval green glass bead

16" length of 24-gauge silver craft wire
silver tie-tack pin back
basic seed bead supplies (see above)

1 String 20 beads onto the center of the wire. Bend the wire into a loop so the last seed bead on each end are touching. Twist the wires together. Flatten the loop a little with your fingers. String 30 beads onto the wire and repeat for a slightly large center loop. String 20 beads onto the wire and repeat to make another side loop.

2 Bend the wire end so it extends from the center of the loops. String the 16mm bead onto the wire. Repeat step 1 to form the other side of the brooch. Wrap the wire end between the loops to secure. Bend the side loops so they extend toward the center as shown. Glue the pin to the back of the 16mm bead.

Multi-strand Bracelet

length: 7½"
seed beads: 220 iridescent
    purple (2.5 grams),
    384 turquoise (4.5 grams)
iridescent purple bugle beads:
    (Katie used 80)
nine 7" lengths of flexible
    beading wire

6 silver crimp tubes
2 silver 3-strand end pieces
silver lobster clasp
wire nippers
chain nose pliers
basic seed bead supplies (see
    page 32)

1 Hold three lengths of wire together and string a crimp tube ½" from the ends. Place the wire end through an outer loop on an end piece and place the wire ends back through the crimp tube; flatten it closed (see page 18).

2 String turquoise beads onto one strand except for ½" on the end. Tape the strand to your work surface to hold the beads in place while you work. On the other two strands, string a mix of purple seed and bugle beads except for ½" on the end. String a crimp tube onto all three strands. Place the wire ends through a loop on the other end piece and back into the crimp tube; flatten it closed. Use the chain nose pliers to help hold the wires if necessary.

3 Attach three wire lengths to each of the remaining loops on the first end piece using the technique in

step 1. On the center set of wires, string two strands of turquoise beads and one of purple beads. Attach them to the center loop on the end piece. On the remaining outer strands string one strand of turquoise beads and two of purple beads. Attach them to the remaining loop on the end piece.

Hair Clip

silver-lined seed beads: 280 pink (3.5 grams), 96 clear (1.5 grams)
8mm clear faceted glass bead
silver craft wire: 24" length of 24-gauge, 18" length of 28-gauge
2¼" clip barrette with a hole at each end
wire nippers
chain nose pliers
basic seed bead supplies (see page 32)

1 String 40 pink beads onto the center of the 24-gauge wire. Bend the wire into a loop so the last beads on each end are touching. Twist the wires together. Repeat, alternating wire ends to make a total of five petals. Adjust the petal shapes with your fingers.

2 String 20 pink beads onto alternating wire ends to make four petals as in step 1.

3 String the faceted bead onto the longest end of the wire. Wrap the wire end around the flower center and twist the two wire ends together at the back of the flower. The free ends should be ½"-1" long.

4 Place one end of the 28-gauge wire through the hole in one end of the barrette and wrap it three times. Wrap the wire around the wide end of the barrette three times. String four clear beads and wrap the wire around the barrette. Repeat until the barrette is covered. Wrap the wire around the barrette three times, then through the hole three times. Trim any excess wire and press the ends to the barrette with chain nose pliers.

5 Place the flower over the barrette, wrap the wires around the center and twist together to secure. Trim any excess wire and press the ends to the barrette with chain nose pliers.

Daisy Chain Necklace

length: 15½''
seed beads: 150 silver (2 grams), 140 iridescent purple (2 grams)
fourteen 4mm round silver beads
65" length of beading thread
silver torpedo clasp
basic seed bead supplies (see page 32)

1 Fold the thread in half. Tie the folded end into a square knot (see page 26) attaching one half of the clasp.

2 String 10 silver seed beads, six purple beads and a 4mm silver bead. Thread the needle through the first purple bead, then string four more purple beads. Thread the needle through the last purple bead in the first set to create the daisy (see diagram). Make a total of 14 daisies with 10 silver seed beads between each. Attach the other half of the clasp with a square knot.

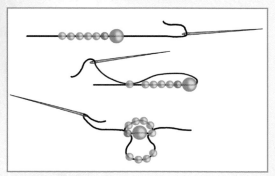

Daisy Chain Bracelet

length: 7¼''
180 pink seed beads (2 grams)
18 white e-beads
48" length of beading thread
gold barrel clasp
basic seed bead supplies (see page 32)

1 Fold the thread in half. Tie the folded end into a square knot (see page 26) attaching one half of the clasp.

2 String six pink beads and a white bead. Thread the needle through the first pink bead, then string four more pink beads. Thread the needle through the last pink bead in the first set to create the daisy (see diagram). Make a total of 18 daisies. Attach the other half of the clasp with a square knot.

Seed Bead Bottle

seed beads: approximately 770 turquoise (9 grams), 1,920 blue (21.5 grams)
4" clear glass bottle
4⅞ yard length of beading thread
turquoise rhinestones: six 6mm round, six 8mm rectangular
8mm blue glass bead
silver head pin
basic seed bead supplies (see page 32)

1 Place 12 drops of glue evenly spaced around the bottle 2" from the bottom edge. Press a rhinestone into each dot, alternating shapes.

2 Cut a 1⅓-yards length of thread. Double knot one end, string turquoise beads except for the last 2" of thread and double knot the end. Use your fingers to cover the bottle above the rhinestones with a thick coat of glue. Wrap the beads around the bottle starting just below the top edge. Cut off any extra strung beads and reknot the end. Place a dot of glue on each knotted end.

3 Cut a 3⅓-yard length of thread and repeat step 2 wrapping the beads around the bottle starting just below the rhinestones.

4 String the 8mm blue bead onto the head pin. Make a wrapped loop (see page 7). String 4" of blue seed beads on an 8" length of thread. String the beaded head pin onto the center of the beaded thread. Wrap the beaded thread around the neck of the bottle and tie the ends into a square knot (see page 26).

Covered Wood Bead Lariat

length: 50"
approximately 900 silver-lined purple
*   seed beads (10 grams)*
two 20mm unfinished wood beads
four 6mm round silver beads
2 silver crimp beads

2 yards of beading thread
48" length of flexible beading wire
chopstick or knitting needle
adhesive tape
basic seed bead supplies (see page 32)

1 Cut the thread in half. Tie a double knot in one end and string seed beads until the thread is covered except for the last 2". Double knot the end of the thread. Place a wood bead on the chopstick and use your finger to cover the bead with a thick coat of glue. Do not cover the holes with glue. Starting at one hole wrap the strung beads around the wood bead until the entire bead is covered. Repeat for the other wood bead; let dry.

2 Place a piece of tape 1½" from one end of the beading wire. String seed beads onto the wire except for 1½" at each end. Remove the tape from one end and string a silver bead, a wood bead, a silver bead and a crimp bead. Flatten the crimp bead closed (see page 18). Repeat for the other end of the wire.

Take The Next Step with Katie

Take The Next Step with Katie

"Come with me as we take the beading experience to the next level. By combining the techniques you've learned in the previous sections, you can achieve amazing results. Some of the designs have beading patterns that are a little more advanced, but they are still projects you can complete in a weekend."

Memory Wire Cuff Bracelet

length: 6½"
3 separate loops of bracelet memory wire
30 assorted 6-10mm black, brown, gold glass beads
72 assorted brown, black, gold e-beads
4 gold 3-hole spacer bars
six 6mm gold memory wire end caps
2-step epoxy glue
memory wire shears
basic next step supplies (see above)

1 Glue an end cap on one end of each of the wire loops. String four assorted e-beads onto each wire. String each wire through a spacer bar. String eight assorted e-beads onto each wire.

2 String each wire through a spacer bar. String 3" of 6-10mm beads onto each wire. String each wire through a spacer bar. String eight assorted e-beads onto each wire. String each wire through a spacer bar. String four assorted e-beads onto each wire. Glue an end cap onto each wire end.

Double-Strand Illusion Necklace

length: 15"
fifteen 8mm clear faceted teardrop beads
30 gold seed beads
48" length of clear nylon line

2 gold crimp beads
gold magnetic clasp
jewelry glue
basic next step supplies (see above)

1 Cut the nylon line in half. Hold two ends together and string a crimp bead ½" from the ends. Place the ends through one half of the clasp and back through the crimp tube; flatten it closed (see page 18) on a single strand. Leave 1" and string a seed bead, a teardrop bead and a seed bead. Thread the line back through the teardrop and the first seed bead. Repeat for a total of eight with 2" between each.

2 On the other strand start the beading pattern from step 1 2" from the clasp. When both strands are complete string a crimp bead on them, attach the other half of the clasp and flatten the crimp bead closed.

Woven Bracelet

length: 6"
four 16mm sterling silver tube beads
round silver beads: twenty-four 4mm, 4 large-hole 6mm,
* 30 small-hole 6mm*
24" length of flexible beading wire
2 silver crimp beads
silver toggle clasp
basic next step supplies (see page 37)

2 String three small-hole beads onto each strand, then string the wire ends through opposite sides of a tube bead. Repeat until all of the tube and beads are used. String the wire ends through opposite sides of a large-hole bead.

3 String four 4mm beads onto each strand. String the wire ends through opposite sides of a large-hole bead. String four 4mm beads and a crimp bead onto each strand.

4 String the wire ends through opposite sides of the other half of the clasp and through the crimp bead on each side of the clasp. Flatten each crimp bead (see page 18).

1 String half of the clasp onto the center of the wire. String four 4mm beads onto each side of the clasp. String the wire ends through opposite sides of a large-hole bead. Adjust the wire so the ends are even. String four 4mm bead onto each strand. String the wire ends through opposite ends of a large-hole bead.

Beaded Pendant on a Chain

length: 20" with pendant
twelve 6mm faceted light blue glass beads
twelve assorted 4mm dark blue glass beads
six 4mm faceted gray glass beads
60 silver seed beads
6mm large-hole silver rondelle
1" silver moon charm
18" silver ball chain necklace
12" length of flexible beading wire
6 silver crimp beads
silver jump rings: one 6mm, one 9mm
basic next step supplies (see page 37)

1 Cut the wire into three equal lengths. Flatten a crimp bead (see page 18) on one end of each length. String a light blue, dark blue, gray, dark blue, light blue and 4-9 seed beads on each length. String each wire through the rondelle. String five seed beads onto each length, fold the wires in a loop and string them back through the rondelle. Repeat the beading pattern in reverse.

2 Attach the pendant to the 9mm jump ring. Connect the 9mm to the 6mm jump ring and string the 6mm onto the necklace. Connect the moon to the 6mm jump ring.

Jump Ring Necklace

length: 21" with pendant
14mm purple/green glass marble
40 iridescent seed beads
14mm gold filigree bell cap
gold chain: 1" length, two 5" length
40 gold jump rings

4 gold split rings
gold lobster clasp
jewelry glue
basic next step supplies (see page 37)

1 Glue the bell cap to the marble and let dry. Connect a split ring to each end of the 1" length of chain. Attach the bell cap to one end of the chain.

2 Form two chains of 20 jump rings each. As you attach the jump rings, place a seed bead on each one. Connect one end of each jump ring chain to the split ring at the top of the 1" chain.

3 Attach a 5" length of chain to each jump ring chain. Attach a split ring to each end of the necklace and the clasp to a split ring.

Gold Spacer Bracelet

length: 7¼"
twenty-six 5mm amethyst bicone glass beads
36 iridescent purple seed beads
twenty-six 4mm round gold beads
fourteen 22mm curved gold spacer tubes
three 7½" lengths of flexible gold beading wire
twenty-six ½" gold head pins
6 gold crimp beads
gold filigree snap clasp for 3 strands
basic next step supplies (see page 37)

1 String each bicone bead onto a separate head pin and make a simple loop (see page 7). Set them aside for steps 2 and 3. String a crimp bead ½" from the end of each wire. String a loop on half of the clasp onto each wire and place the end back into the crimp bead; flatten each closed (see page 18).

2 For each outer strand string a tube, a seed bead, a round gold, two beaded head pins, a round gold and a seed bead. Repeat for a total of four sets. String a tube and a crimp bead. String the wire through the corresponding hole on the other half of the clasp and back into the crimp bead; flatten it closed.

3 For the center strand string two seed beads, a round gold, two beaded head pins, a round gold, two seed beads and a tube. Repeat for a total of four sets. String two seed beads, a round gold, two beaded head pins, a round gold, two seed beads, a tube and a crimp bead. String the wire through the corresponding hole on the other half of the clasp and back into the crimp bead; flatten it closed.

Gemstone Doughnut Necklace

AB finish = Aurora Borealis is a rainbow-like finish added to glass beads

length: 18" with pendant
35mm amethyst/fluorite gemstone doughnut
amethyst beads: two 6mm round, eight chips, four 4mm round
black glass beads: four 8mm bicone, four 6mm AB finish* faceted
28 black seed beads
eight 8mm silver bead caps

10½" length of flexible beading wire
12" length of 1mm black leather cord
6" length of 24-gauge silver craft wire
3 silver crimp beads
2 silver eye crimps
2 silver split rings
silver spring ring clasp
basic next step supplies (see page 37)

1 Cut the leather and the craft wire in half. Attach an eye crimp (see page 18) to one end of each length of leather. Connect a split ring to each eye crimp and attach the clasp to one split ring. On the free end of each length of leather, fold ¾" back and wrap a 3" length of wire around it. Use chain nose pliers to press the wire ends into the leather. Pull gently to make sure each loop is secure.

2 Cut a 4" length of beading wire and string the seed beads and a crimp bead onto it. Thread it through the center of the gemstone doughnut. String the wire end through the opposite side of the crimp bead and carefully flatten it closed without breaking any seed beads.

3 String a crimp bead ½" from one end of a 6½" length of beading wire. String the wire through the leather loop and back into the crimp bead; flatten it closed. String a faceted black bead, a 4mm amethyst, a faceted black, a 4mm amethyst, a bead cap, a black bicone, a bead cap, four amethyst chips, a bead cap, a black bicone, bead cap and a 6mm amethyst. String the seed bead loop and repeat the beading pattern in the reverse order. String a crimp bead and the remaining leather loop. Place the wire end back into the crimp bead and flatten it closed.

Double-Strand Necklace

length: 19" with charm
clear faceted glass beads:
    one hundred forty-three 4mm,
    sixteen 8mm
20 clear seed beads
sixty 4mm silver rondelles
flexible beading wire: 17" and 19" lengths

1" silver key charm
4 silver crimp beads
6mm silver jump ring
2 silver split rings
silver spring ring clasp
basic next step supplies (see page 37)

1 String a crimp bead ½" from one end of the 17" length of wire. String a split ring and place the wire end back into the crimp bead; flatten it closed (see page 18). String a rondelle and three 4mm beads; repeat for a total of 29 times. String a rondelle and a crimp bead. Place the wire through a split ring and back into the crimp bead; flatten it closed.

2 String a crimp bead ½" from one end of the 19" length of wire. String a split ring from the beaded 17" wire and place the wire end back into the crimp bead; flatten it closed. String 10 seed beads. String a rondelle and six 4mm beads; repeat for a total of three sets. String a rondelle, a 10mm, a rondelle, a 10mm, a rondelle and three 4mm beads; repeat for total of three sets. String a rondelle, a 10mm, a rondelle, a 10mm, a rondelle and a 4mm bead. Attach the charm to the jump ring and string it onto the wire. Repeat step 2 in the reverse order. Attach the clasp to one of the split rings.